festive picnics

festive picnics

recipes by
PAMELA SHELDON JOHNS

crafts by
JENNIFER BARRY DESIGN

photography by
JOYCE OUDKERK-POOL

TEN SPEED PRESS
BERKELEY · TORONTO

A Kirsty Melville Book

Ten Speed Press
Box 7123
Berkeley, California 94707
www.tenspeed.com

Distributed in Australia by Simon & Schuster Australia, in Canada by Ten Speed Press Canada,
in New Zealand by Southern Publishers Group, in South Africa by Real Books, in Southeast Asia by Berkeley Books,
and in the United Kingdom and Europe by Airlift Book Company.

Concept and Design: Jennifer Barry Design, Fairfax, California
Photography: Joyce Oudkerk-Pool, San Francisco, California
Layout Production: Kristen Wurz
Copy Editor: Carolyn Miller
Food Stylist: Pouké Halpern
Prop Stylist: Carol Hacker/Tableprop, San Francisco
Proofreader: Beverly McGuire

Library of Congress Cataloging-in-Publication Data
Johns, Pamela Sheldon, 1953–
Festive picnics : recipes, crafts, and decorations for outdoor occasions/
recipes by Pamela Sheldon Johns ; crafts by Jennifer Barry Design ;
photography by Joyce Oudkerk-Pool.
p.   cm.
Includes index.
ISBN 1-58008-560-1 (pbk.)
1. Outdoor cookery.   2. Picnicking.
I. Barry, Jennifer.   II. Title.
TX823 .J52 2004
641.5'78—dc22   2003019703

Printed in China

10 9 8 7 6 5 4 3 2 1 – 08 07 06 05 04

Acknowledgments

Pamela Sheldon Johns: I would like to thank my fellow picnic mates, Alaia and Courtney, for their love and support (and willingness to taste everything!). Thank you to Caroline Baratta and Norman Jaffe for their help with recipe testing, to Carolyn Miller for her meticulous copyediting, and to Joyce Oudkerk-Pool and Pouké Halpern for creating beautiful images from my words. Most of all, I send love and respect to my wise and crafty friend, Jennifer Barry. It has been, as always, a picnic working with her.

Jennifer Barry: I would like to thank the following individuals for their help on this book project: Ten Speed publisher Kirsty Melville, for her support and early encouragement to do a picnic book; editor Meghan Keeffe and production manager Hal Hershey, for shepherding the book to its beautiful finished state; my coauthor and friend Pamela Sheldon Johns, who has inspired me in countless ways on so many projects and hosted many memorable and delicious meals *al fresco*; photographer Joyce Oudkerk-Pool, food stylist Pouké Halpern, and prop stylist Carol Hacker, for creating such beautiful photography and for being so much fun to work with that it never seems like work; my friend and design production colleague Kristen Wurz, for being the best there is at everything she does; Leslie Anne Barry, for her help with the early design of this book; photography assistant Stephanie Coyner, food-styling assistant Jeff Larsen, photography production assistants Chloé Halpern and James Cabrera, and models Skylar Drake and Max Oudkerk-Pool; Adolph Gasser Incorporated for equipment rentals; and special thanks to Jane Bay for allowing us to photograph in her lovely home and garden.

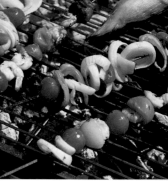

Introduction

Whether you are watching fireworks on the tailgate of a pickup truck and drinking strawberry-mint lemonade, or warming your toes by a campfire while sipping cocoa and munching on brownies, almost any occasion is an excellent excuse for dining away from the traditional table. A portable meal seems to taste even better when accompanied with a fresh mountain breeze, the blaze of a sunset, or the aroma of salt water.

With a little advance planning, a delicious picnic can be taken on a road trip in the car, camping, cross-country skiing, or to a concert, sporting event, or pool party. Even indoor meals can have the ambience of a picnic; try a winter brunch in a sunny room or a cozy dinner in front of the fireplace. And, the most appreciated picnic of all may be the one you bring with you on an airplane.

Thinking Outside the Lunch Box

Picnics can run the gamut from a formal affair with chairs and table settings of fine china and crystal to a casual, impromptu spread of bread, cheese, and wine. Whether you transport the food in a picnic basket or a backpack, you can add a new twist to the classic outdoor meal when you organize a potluck picnic, or one based on a theme, such as a Mother's Day afternoon tea or a Fourth of July barbecue. Picnics are ideal for birthday parties,

too; gone are the worries about spills and drips, and the whole outdoors is available for play before and after the meal.

The word *pique-nique* dates back to the end of the seventeenth century in France. *Pique* means "to pick," or perhaps "nibble," and *nique* is probably just a nonsense rhyming word. By the mid-1700s, the word was found in German as *Picknick*. By the early 1800s, it made its way to England. The definition was a box lunch or potluck meal, often in conjunction with a religious gathering. In modern use, a picnic is an outing with food. Because of the pleasant association, the word is also used to describe a pleasant or easy task: "That should be a picnic!"

Getting Ready

Preparation is the key to a successful picnic. Whether you are going all out with decorations and an elaborate menu or just spreading a blanket, you don't want to forget any key elements—such as forks to eat with or matches for the grill. Charcoal grills impart the best flavor and aroma to the food. However, for more elaborate events, you can set up an outdoor kitchen with such modern conveniences as gas grills and refrigeration. Away from home, there are even propane-powered blenders, appliance adapters that plug into the cigarette lighter of the car, and portable propane grills that clip onto the tailgate of a pickup truck.

Setting the Table (or Blanket)

How will you eat your picnic? Silverware, plates, cups, and glasses are now all available in paper or single-use plastic. Disposable items are convenient, but there are other environmentally friendly options. Try using heavier reuseable plastic or enameled tin plates, or, depending on your venue, use your regular flatware and dishes straight from your kitchen. Sometimes the food seems to taste better when eaten from a regular plate. For Asian menus, chopsticks are nice to bring along. If you are picnicking in a place that is known for wind, consider weights for your napkins and tablecloth (see page 66). Think up some fun ways to serve food, such as in baskets or our decorated sand pails on page 42. And don't forget to bring serving utensils for each dish.

The decision whether to use a table and chairs or simply spread out a blanket or tablecloth on a tailgate will be determined by the menu, the theme, and the setting. In any case, be sure to consider decorative elements such as vases for collecting wildflowers. Ambience is always important, so you may want to bring along a few CDs and some candles.

Keeping It Cool or Hot: Food Safety

Once you have prepared your food, you need to package it for safe travel. Given the opportunity, bacteria will grow in certain foods if not stored properly. It is important to keep hot foods hot and cold foods cold. The trouble occurs in foods left between 40°F and 140°F, particularly if they are left in that temperature range for more than an hour. The most susceptible foods are meats, poultry, eggs, and mayonnaise.

There are a number of containers on the market for transporting food. Thermoses come in all sizes, as do coolers. Besides the classic Styrofoam or thermal ice chests, some have wheels or are collapsible or battery powered, others plug into a car's cigarette lighter, and some even have built-in radios. An ice chest can also be used to transport hot dishes. Line it with a heavy towel and pack the food piping hot. Fill the chest as full as possible as airspace dissipates heat.

When preparing picnic food, take special care. Be sure that cooked dishes that will be served chilled have cooled completely and have had time to chill well in the refrigerator before packing them in the ice chest. Pack hot food in a Thermos or an insulated container if you are not using an ice chest to transport the food. As an extra safety measure, sterilize containers with boiling water before filling with hot food.

For cold foods, try to estimate exact portions so that you don't have to feel guilty about tossing leftovers, because unless you have kept the food well chilled it won't be safe to eat after a day outside. Bring plenty of ice. If you have space in the ice chest use the blue plastic cold packs that are to be kept in your freezer specifically for using in ice chests. Or fill the chest with plastic bottles of water that have been frozen, they will help keep it cool, and at the end of the day will provide a refreshing drink.

At the picnic site, keep your cooler of food in the shade and open it as seldom as possible. Keep drinks in a bucket of ice or in a second ice chest.

Cooking Away from Home

Outdoor cooking is an art, even at its simplest. If you have a metal rack, such as an oven rack, you can collect a few stones or stack some bricks, and presto, an instant grill! Nowadays, there are all kinds of portable cooking devices as well, from simple backpacking stoves and hibachis to propane whole-turkey fryers. Whatever apparatus you choose, there are some basics to remember.

In live-fire grills, charcoal, rather than wood, is the most consistent source of heat for cooking. Charcoal briquettes, especially those billed as quick lighting, are made with chemicals that impart fumes, and off flavors, to your food. Look for hardwood charcoal instead. Be sure to bring something to start the fire. Paper and kindling are the best, as fire starters have the same off-putting chemical smells as their chemically produced charcoal briquette counterparts. Chimney starters that use wadded-up newspapers are very handy. And don't forget the matches!

A spray bottle filled with water is excellent for controlling flareups. A box of baking soda is a good safety measure in case the fire gets out of hand. The smoke from aromatic wood chips such as hickory or mesquite or grapevine cuttings adds heavenly flavors to grilling food. They work best if soaked in water, then scattered over the coals just before the food is placed on the grill.

Pack a grilling toolbox that will be ready to go at the drop of a sunhat. At the minimum, it should contain matches, a couple of pot holders, long-handled tongs, a long-handled spatula, a long-handled fork, and a baster or basting brush. It should also contain a spray water bottle, a box of baking soda, aluminum foil, and a wire brush to clean the grill. Other items to bring along include a cutting board, a sharp knife for chopping, a carving knife, a meat thermometer, skewers, corn-cob holders, bottle stoppers, and trash bags. It is good to always have charcoal and some hickory or mesquite chips on hand; you never know when you will have the urge for an impromptu barbecue (also see our grilling checklist on page 12).

Cooking on a Grill

To keep food from sticking, be sure the grill grids are clean, hot, and oiled before placing meat or vegetables on them. Once the meat or vegetables are on the grill, don't move them for at least 30 seconds.

To be sure that bacteria are destroyed, cook poultry and meat such as hamburgers and steaks to 160°F (medium doneness). In both cases, if you don't have a meat thermometer, check for doneness by piercing the thickest part of the food and checking to see that the juices run clear, not pink. After the food is cooked, poultry in particular should not be put back on the plate that held the raw food, as this can cause contamination from bacteria in the uncooked juices. For the same reason, marinades used for raw meat, chicken, or fish should not be used. If you want to baste with marinades, or use some as a condiment, set some aside before it has contact with the uncooked meat, or boil any used marinade for 5 minutes.

Cleanup

Cleaning up can be relatively easy if you come prepared. After reusable plates have been scraped, they can be rinsed in a small dishpan, then tied up in trash bags to take home for washing. Leftover food should be tossed unless you are certain it has been held at a proper temperature. Once home, clean coolers with a water and baking soda solution to eliminate odors and leave them open to dry well.

While the grill is still hot, clean the grids with a wire brush. If some food sticks, soak the grill rack in water and baking soda solution when you get home.

Before You Go

Don't forget to check the weather. Wind or sudden thunderstorms can ruin your well-laid plans. If it is very hot, bring along a tent, canopy, or umbrella, not just for people, but also to keep food cool. Those famous picnic ants need to be checked for before setting down stakes. Small mesh table tents are great deterrents for flies and yellow jackets, and citronella candles will help repel mosquitoes after dark.

A Picnic Packing List

While you may not need everything on this list, it will help to remind you of a few essentials.

- Eating utensils
- Plates
- Cups, glasses
- Napkins
- Toothpicks
- Serving dishes and baskets; utensils for each dish
- Cutting board and chopping knife
- Can opener, bottle opener, corkscrew
- Ice and ice chests or coolers
- Table, chairs, and tablecloth or blanket
- Insect issues: citronella candles, mesh table tents
- Lighting: candles, luminarias
- Entertainment: fishing pole, Frisbee, croquet, radio, guitar
- Food and beverages (don't forget water)
- Extra nibbles: olives, cheeses, crackers, chips and dips, fruit, crudités, baguette
- Condiments: salt, pepper, and sugar
- First-aid kit, flashlight, sunscreen

Grilling Checklist

- Grill (if using propane, check gas)
- Charcoal
- Paper and kindling or fire starter
- Matches
- Wood chips
- Spray water bottle
- Box of baking soda
- Grilling tools:
    - Pot holder, oven mitt
    - Long-handled tongs, spatula, and fork
    - Baster or basting brush
    - Aluminum foil
- Cleanup supplies:
    - Wire brush to clean grill
    - Paper towels, cloth towels
    - Sponge or dishcloth, soap, and dishpan
    - Trash bags
    - Containers for leftovers; bottle stoppers

Festive Picnic Menus

It doesn't take a lot to make a holiday picnic special. A few baskets, colorful tablecloths, and fresh flowers will make a great backdrop for your outdoor event. A late spring tea is charming with tea sandwiches and sweets placed on a serving tray lined with green grassy sod. A date to a concert will be more romantic when the brownies are presented on a bed of pink rose petals. Set up a table with stuffed bears for a teddy bear picnic for a child's birthday. The following are some theme menus for special holidays, and in the following pages you will find other ideas for decorating your picnic.

Asian

Here are some wonderful do-ahead dishes that feature Asian ingredients. In keeping with the theme, take chopsticks along.

Asian Coleslaw
Grilled Sesame Chicken Sandwiches with
Wasabi Mayonnaise and Radish Sprouts
Enoki Cucumber Rolls
Iced Green Tea Spritzers

Fourth of July

Uncle Sam would be proud of this old-fashioned menu. The coleslaw and tartlets can be made earlier in the day. Bring the corn and hamburgers ready to cook.

Garlicky Barbecued Corn
Grilled Hamburgers
Old-Fashioned Coleslaw
Red, White, and Blue Tartlets
Strawberry-Mint Lemonade

Fiesta

This is the perfect poolside menu, a colorful combination of seasonal fruits, vegetables, and spices. Everything but the salmon can be prepared ahead.

Corn, Roasted Pepper, and Arugula Salad
Grilled Salmon Fillets with Pepper-Papaya Chutney
Minted Orange and Mango Salad
Banana Cake with Blueberry Sauce
Lime-Cooler Margaritas
Sangría

Outdoor Concert Picnic in the Grass

Elegant and easy, these dishes taste even better with a concert in the background. Transport the gazpacho in an insulated Thermos to keep it nice and cold.

Gazpacho
Creamy Tarragon Chicken Salad
Black and White Chocolate Brownies

Mother's Day Afternoon Tea

Set up a table outdoors on the patio and treat Mom to a special event. Everything can be made ahead and served in decorated baskets, as described on page 45.

Cold Avocado and Cucumber Soup
Goat Cheese, Arugula, and Tapenade Tea Sandwiches
or
Shrimp and Fennel Salad in Mini Pita Pockets
Raspberry Scones

Beach Party

Cool off with this homage to sun and sea. If you don't want to grill at the beach, prepare the kabobs at home and refrigerate them to transport. Once at the beach, let them warm up a little before serving.

Mediterranean Marinated Swordfish and Shrimp Kabobs
Couscous Salad
Apple-Zucchini Cake
Honey-Orange Sun Tea

Bike/Hike Picnic

Working up an appetite? Lean your bike up against a park bench, and recover your energy with these ready-to-eat sandwiches. See pages 32 and 35 for fun ways to package the sandwiches.

Avocado, Pecorino, and Watercress Baguettes
or
Hummus and Pickled Onion Sandwich Wraps
Meyer Lemon Squares

Father's Day Mixed Italian Grill

Here is a hearty tribute to Dad. After the appetizer of prosecco and crostini, break out a bold red wine to accompany the grilled food.

Prosecco-Cassis Spritzers
Grilled Prosciutto-Wrapped Figs on Gorgonzola Crostini
Split and Skewered Grilled Game Hens with Chili-Orange Glaze
Grilled Italian Sausage Skewers with Onion and Sweet Pepper
Roasted New Potato Salad with Pancetta-Rosemary Dressing
Cheesecake with Brandied Cherries

soups, salads, & sandwiches

2

Cold Avocado and Cucumber Soup

THIS PALE GREEN SOUP IS PRETTY TO LOOK AT AND REFRESHINGLY COOL ON A HOT SUMMER DAY.

1 ripe avocado

Juice of 1/2 lemon

1 English (hothouse) cucumber, peeled, seeded, and diced

2 cups plain yogurt

1 green onion (including 1 inch of the green part),
finely chopped

1-1/2 teaspoons minced fresh tarragon

1/2 cup fat-free canned chicken broth

Salt and freshly ground white pepper to taste

4 radishes, thinly sliced

With a large, sharp knife, cut the avocado in half lengthwise and remove the seed by striking its center quickly with the middle part of the knife and twisting the seed clockwise a half turn. Scoop out the flesh with a large serving spoon. Each half can then be sliced. Set aside one-fourth of the slices for garnish, sprinkling with the lemon juice to keep the avocado from turning dark.

In a blender, combine the remaining avocado, the cucumber, yogurt, green onion, and tarragon. Purée until smooth. Add broth to the desired consistency and season with salt and pepper. Cover and refrigerate for at least two hours before serving. Garnish with the reserved avocado and the radish slices just before serving. *Serves 6*

Gazpacho

THE PERFECT SUMMER DISH, REFRESHING AND VIBRANT WITH RIPE TOMATOES AND COOL CUCUMBERS.

1 red bell pepper, seeded, deribbed,
and coarsely chopped

1 green bell pepper, seeded, deribbed,
and coarsely chopped

1 English (hothouse) cucumber, peeled and diced

1 pound ripe tomatoes, peeled and coarsely chopped
(see note)

2 slices day-old bread, crusts removed,
soaked in water for 5 minutes, then squeezed dry

2 cloves garlic

2 green onions (including 1 inch of the green part),
finely chopped

2 tablespoons olive oil

1 tablespoon sherry wine vinegar

1/2 teaspoon sweet Hungarian paprika

Salt and freshly ground black pepper

Minced fresh parsley, for garnish

In a blender or food processor, combine the red bell pepper, green bell pepper, cucumber, and tomatoes. Add the bread, garlic, green onions, oil, vinegar, and paprika and process until smooth. Season with salt and pepper.

Cover and refrigerate for at least 2 hours, or overnight, before serving. Ladle into chilled bowls and garnish with a sprinkle of parsley. *Serves 6*

TO PEEL TOMATOES: Remove the core from each tomato. Drop in boiling water for 30 seconds; transfer immediately to ice water to stop the cooking and release the skins. The peel will slip off in your hands. To seed, cut the tomatoes in half and squeeze out the seeds.

18

Chili

PERFECT FOR A COOL WEATHER OR EVENING PICNIC, THIS CHILI NEEDS TO BE STARTED A DAY AHEAD.

FOR A QUICKER VERSION, SUBSTITUTE CANNED KIDNEY AND WHITE BEANS, USING ONE 15-OUNCE CAN FOR EACH

1/2 CUP DRIED BEANS. COMBINE WITH THE LENTILS AND COOK FOR JUST 30 MINUTES.

1/2 cup dried red kidney beans

1/2 cup dried white beans

1/2 cup olive oil

2 large carrots, peeled and cut into
1/2-inch-wide slices

3 stalks celery, cut into 1/2-inch-wide slices

2 onions, chopped into 1/2-inch pieces

3 cloves garlic, minced

2 (16-ounce) cans whole tomatoes

8 cups canned low-salt chicken broth

1 tablespoon ground cumin

2 tablespoons minced fresh oregano

2 tablespoons pure chili powder

1/2 cup dried lentils

Salt and freshly ground black pepper

Cayenne pepper

Rinse and pick over the red and white beans. Soak in water to cover overnight. Drain.

In a large stockpot, over medium heat, heat the oil and add the carrots, celery, onions, and garlic. Sauté for 3 to 4 minutes, or until softened. Add the tomatoes and their juices and the broth and bring to a boil.

Add the red and white beans, cumin, oregano, and chili powder. Reduce the temperature to a simmer and cook for 1-1/2 hours, or until the beans have softened slightly. Add the lentils and cook an additional 30 minutes, or until the beans and lentils are tender. Season with salt, pepper, and cayenne to taste. *Serves 6*

19

Roasted New Potato Salad
with Pancetta-Rosemary Dressing

PANCETTA IS A FLAVORFUL MEAT THAT DERIVES ITS NAME FROM *PANCIA*—ITALIAN FOR "BELLY."
IT IS MADE BY RUBBING A SLAB OF PORK BELLY WITH A MIXTURE OF SPICES AND CURING IT FOR
TWO MONTHS OR LONGER. BACON CAN BE SUBSTITUTED.

2 pounds new potatoes, scrubbed and halved

6 tablespoons extra-virgin olive oil

Salt and freshly ground black pepper

1 onion, diced

4 ounces pancetta, diced

1/4 cup red wine vinegar

1 teaspoon Dijon mustard

3/4 cup extra-virgin olive oil

3 tablespoons minced fresh rosemary

Preheat the oven to 400°F. Toss the potatoes with 4 tablespoons of the olive oil and place in a roasting pan. Season with salt and pepper. Spread in the roasting pan and roast, turning occasionally, until golden brown and fork tender, about 20 minutes. Set aside to cool.

In a small sauté pan, heat 2 tablespoons of the olive oil over medium heat and sauté the onion and pancetta 3 to 4 minutes, or until lightly browned. Set aside to cool.

In a large bowl, combine the vinegar and mustard. While constantly whisking, drizzle in the remaining 3/4 cup olive oil. Add the onion and pancetta mixture and rosemary. Add the potatoes and toss to coat well. *Serves 6*

Corn, Roasted Pepper, and Arugula Salad

WHEN ROASTED, PEPPERS BECOME SOFT AND SWEET, PERFECT WITH SWEET CORN AND PEPPERY ARUGULA.

DRESSING

2 tablespoons red wine vinegar

6 tablespoons extra-virgin olive oil

Salt and freshly ground black pepper

2 red bell peppers, roasted and cut lengthwise into
1-inch-wide strips (see note)

2 yellow bell peppers, roasted and cut lengthwise into
1-inch-wide strips (see note)

1/2 cup sliced red onion

2 cups arugula

1 cup fresh corn kernels

To make the dressing, pour the vinegar into a glass or stainless-steel bowl. Slowly drizzle in the oil, whisking constantly. Season with salt and pepper to taste.

In a salad bowl or picnic storage container, toss the peppers, onion, arugula, and corn together. Drizzle in the dressing and toss to coat. Serve at room temperature. *Serves 4*

TO ROAST PEPPERS: Place whole peppers directly over a high gas flame. If you do not have a gas stovetop, use a grill or put the peppers on a baking sheet under your broiler. Turn the peppers frequently until blackened all over. Place them in a brown paper bag and let cool. Peel the peppers by scraping the blackened skin off with a sharp knife. Remove the stems, inner ribs, and seeds.

Creamy Tarragon Chicken Salad

THIS TARRAGON DRESSING ALSO MARRIES WELL
WITH SLICED GRILLED STEAK.

2 cups canned low-salt chicken broth

2 boneless, skinless whole chicken breasts

3 tablespoons tarragon vinegar

2 cloves garlic, minced

1 teaspoon Dijon mustard

1/2 cup safflower oil

1/4 cup minced fresh tarragon

Salt and freshly ground black pepper

1/2 cup pitted and halved black olives

Leaves from 1 head curly endive

In a large saucepan, bring the broth to a low simmer. Add the chicken breasts, cover, and poach for 7 to 8 minutes, or until the chicken is firm. Set aside. When cooled, slice the chicken into horizontal slices, place in large bowl, and set aside.

In a large bowl, combine the vinegar, garlic, and mustard. Whisking constantly, slowly drizzle in the oil. Stir in the tarragon and season with salt and pepper.

In a large bowl, toss the chicken slices, dressing, and olives together. Serve on a bed of endive. *Serves 4*

Old-Fashioned Coleslaw

THIS CLASSIC COLESLAW HAS A CREAMY DRESSING. BE SURE
TO KEEP IT WELL CHILLED UNTIL READY TO SERVE,
UP TO 2 HOURS IN ADVANCE. IF MADE TOO FAR AHEAD, THE
COLESLAW WILL BECOME LIQUIDY.

1 pound cabbage, cored and shredded (8 cups)

1 carrot, peeled and shredded

1/4 cup sliced green onions
(including 1 inch of the green part)

3 tablespoons cider vinegar

1/2 cup mayonnaise

1/4 cup sugar

1 teaspoon dry mustard

1 teaspoon celery seed

Salt and freshly ground black pepper

In a large bowl, combine the cabbage, carrot, and green onions. In a small bowl, combine the vinegar, mayonnaise, sugar, dry mustard, and celery seed. Stir to blend. Season with salt and pepper. Pour the dressing over the cabbage mixture and stir well to coat. Cover and refrigerate until ready to serve. *Serves 8*

Asian Coleslaw

TOASTED-PEANUT OIL, FOUND IN ASIAN GROCERY STORES,
ADDS AN INTERESTING FLAVOR DIMENSION TO THIS SALAD.

2 cloves garlic, minced

1 serrano chile, seeded and minced (or more to taste)

3 tablespoons rice vinegar

3 tablespoons freshly squeezed lime juice

2 tablespoons sugar

1 teaspoon Thai green curry paste or curry powder

1/4 cup toasted peanut oil

1 pound napa cabbage, shredded (8 cups)

1 cucumber, peeled, seeded, and diced

5 green onions (including 1 inch of the green part), sliced

3 tablespoons minced fresh cilantro

3 tablespoons minced fresh mint

1/4 cup peanuts, toasted and coarsely chopped

In a large bowl, combine the garlic, chile, rice vinegar, lime juice, sugar, and curry paste. Gradually whisk in the oil.

Add the napa cabbage, cucumber, green onions, and cilantro. Toss to coat and chill in the refrigerator or ice chest. When ready to serve, sprinkle each serving with mint and peanuts. *Serves 8*

Couscous Salad

THIS DISH CAN BE HEATED AS A WINTER SIDE DISH,
OR SERVED CHILLED FOR A SUMMER SALAD.

3 tablespoons extra-virgin olive oil

4 chopped green onions (including 1 inch of the green part)

2 garlic cloves, minced

1 red bell pepper, seeded, deribbed, and finely chopped

1-1/2 cups canned low-salt chicken broth

1/4 cup dried currants

1-1/2 cups couscous

Grated zest and juice of 1/2 lemon

1/4 cup extra-virgin olive oil

Salt and freshly ground black pepper

1 cup cooked garbanzo beans

Romaine lettuce leaves, for garnish

1/4 cup pine nuts, toasted

In a large skillet over medium heat, heat the 3 tablespoons extra-virgin olive oil. Add the onions, garlic, and bell pepper and sauté until tender, about 2 minutes. Add the broth and currants and bring to a boil. Add the couscous, cover, and re-move from the heat. Let stand for 5 minutes.

In a small bowl, whisk the lemon zest, lemon juice, and 1/4 cup olive oil together. Season with salt and pepper.

Fluff the couscous with a fork. Add the garbanzo beans and dressing. Let cool. Place on a bed of lettuce leaves on a serving platter. Sprinkle with the pine nuts to serve. *Serves 6*

Enoki Cucumber Rolls

SLENDER WHITE ENOKI MUSHROOMS ARE FOUND IN SPECIALTY PRODUCE MARKETS AND MANY SUPERMARKETS.

IF UNAVAILABLE, SUBSTITUTE 3 OUNCES MUNG BEAN SPROUTS.

2 cups short-grain rice, rinsed

2-1/4 cups water

1/4 cup rice vinegar

3 tablespoons sugar

1/2 teaspoon salt

1 tablespoon black or
toasted white sesame seeds

3 English (hothouse) cucumbers

1 (4-ounce) package enoki mushrooms
(if not available, substitute bean sprouts)

1 red bell pepper, seeded, deribbed, and
cut into julienne

1 bunch daikon radish sprouts

Soy sauce, for serving

1 tube of prepared wasabi paste

In a medium saucepan, combine the rice and water. Cover tightly, bring to a boil, then reduce heat to low. Cook for 15 minutes; do not open the lid during cooking. Remove from heat. Uncover the pan and quickly spread a tea towel over the rice. Replace the cover and let stand for 15 minutes.

In another saucepan, combine the rice vinegar, sugar, and salt. Place over low heat and cook, stirring, until the sugar is dissolved. Set aside to cool.

Transfer the rice to a large bowl and fluff it with a fork. Add the vinegar mixture and fold it into rice while fanning constantly with a hand fan to cool the mixture. Continue fanning and folding, taking care not to smash the rice grains, until all liquid has been absorbed and the mixture is cool, about 10 minutes.

Moisten your fingers and form the rice into twenty-four 1-inch balls. Squeeze each gently to elongate it and place on a tray; do not stack. Sprinkle with sesame seeds.

With a long, thin-bladed knife or mandoline, cut the cucumbers into very thin lengthwise slices. Place the strips on paper towels and blot dry. Place a rice ball, a few enoki mushrooms, a couple of red pepper strips, and a few daikon sprouts on each slice and roll up. Secure with a toothpick and place on a serving platter, or pack in a picnic storage container and chill before transporting in an ice chest.

When ready to serve, pour a small amount of soy sauce into individual small bowls for each person. Serve with a dab of wasabi for guests to stir into the soy sauce to their own taste. *Serves 8*

Goat Cheese, Arugula, and Tapenade Tea Sandwiches

AN ASSORTMENT OF TEA SANDWICHES MAKES A LOVELY PICNIC. SOME OTHER FILLINGS OR OPEN-FACE TOPPINGS MIGHT INCLUDE CREAM CHEESE AND ROASTED RED BELL PEPPER, PROSCIUTTO AND JULIENNED SUN-DRIED TOMATOES, OR THINLY SLICED CUCUMBER AND SMOKED SALMON.

TAPENADE

1/2 cup oil-cured black olives, pitted

1 tablespoon extra-virgin olive oil

1/3 teaspoon finely grated orange zest

1 cup arugula leaves, coarsely chopped

12 cherry tomatoes, halved

2 tablespoons red wine vinegar

2 tablespoons extra-virgin olive oil

Salt and freshly ground black pepper

8 thin slices white bread, crusts removed

4 ounces fresh goat cheese, at room temperature

To make the tapenade, combine the olives, olive oil, and orange zest in a food processor. Pulse to a smooth paste. Set aside.

In a small bowl, combine the arugula and cherry tomatoes. Drizzle with the vinegar and olive oil. Season with salt and pepper. Toss to coat.

Spread the olive paste on 4 slices of the bread; spread the goat cheese on the 4 remaining slices. Place the arugula mixture on each olive paste slice and top with the goat cheese slices. Cut diagonally into triangles. *Serves 4*

Grilled Sesame Chicken Sandwiches with Wasabi Mayonnaise and Radish Sprouts

WASABI, OR JAPANESE HORSERADISH, CAN BE PURCHASED IN A PASTE OR IN POWDERED FORM.

WASABI POWDER ALLOWS YOU TO ADJUST THE SPICINESS AS YOU LIKE.

2 boneless, skinless whole chicken breasts

1/4 cup soy sauce

1/4 cup dry sherry

2 tablespoons coarse-grained mustard

1 tablespoon honey

1 teaspoon grated fresh ginger

1/2 cup unbleached all-purpose flour

1/2 cup cornstarch

1/2 cup sesame seeds, toasted (see note)

1 cup mayonnaise

1 tablespoon wasabi powder, or to taste

1 green onion (including 1 inch of the green part),
thinly sliced

8 slices country-style bread

1/2 cup daikon radish sprouts

1/4 cup minced fresh cilantro

Cut the chicken breasts lengthwise into 1-inch-wide strips. Thread onto bamboo skewers and set aside.

In a medium bowl, combine the soy sauce, sherry, mustard, honey, and ginger. Stir to blend. Add the chicken. Let stand for at least 1 hour, or cover and refrigerate for as long as overnight.

Light a fire in a charcoal grill or preheat a gas grill to 475°F.

In a small, shallow bowl, combine the flour, cornstarch, and sesame seeds. Stir to blend. Remove the chicken skewers from the marinade. Dredge each skewer in the flour mixture to coat evenly. Grill for about 5 minutes on each side, or until opaque throughout. Set aside to cool. Remove and discard the skewers.

In a small bowl, mix the mayonnaise, wasabi, and green onion together. Spread on each slice of bread. Add a layer of sprouts, then top with the chicken slices and sprinkle with cilantro. *Serves 4*

TO TOAST SEEDS: Place the seeds in a nonstick pan over medium high heat. Cook, stirring frequently, for 3 to 4 minutes, or until the seeds are golden brown. Remove from the pan immediately to cool.

Shrimp and Fennel Salad in Mini Pita Pockets

THE SHRIMP AND FENNEL SALAD IS ALSO SCRUMPTIOUS SERVED ON A BED OF LETTUCE.

8 ounces medium shrimp, shelled

1 bulb fennel, julienned

1 cup assorted sprouts
(such as fennel, daikon, or sunflower)

1 bunch watercress, stemmed

1/4 cup fresh chervil or flat-leaf parsley leaves

1 bunch chives, minced

1 bunch red radishes, coarsely grated

1/4 cup freshly squeezed lemon juice

1/4 cup tarragon vinegar

3/4 cup safflower oil

1 teaspoon finely grated lemon zest

Salt and freshly ground white pepper

6 mini pitas, split

With a thin-bladed knife slice down the back of each shrimp, just deep enough to reveal the dark vein. Remove the vein and rinse the shrimp. Cook the shrimp in salted boiling water for 2 to 3 minutes, or just until pink. Drain.

In a medium bowl, combine the shrimp, fennel, sprouts, watercress, chervil, chives, and radishes. Toss to mix well.

In another medium bowl, combine the lemon juice and vinegar. While whisking constantly, slowly drizzle in the oil. Stir in the lemon zest; season with salt and pepper. Add the vinaigrette to the shrimp mixture and toss well.

If transporting, cover and chill well in the refrigerator before packing in an ice chest. Spoon the filling into the mini pitas when ready to serve. *Serves 6*

Avocado, Pecorino, and Watercress Baguettes

PECORINO IS A SHEEP'S MILK CHEESE FROM ITALY. THE *PECORINO ROMANO* FOUND IN
AMERICAN DELICATESSENS TENDS TO BE AGED LONGER AND IS BEST FOR GRATING. LOOK FOR *PECORINO TOSCANO,*
THE TUSCAN VERSION, WHICH IS YOUNGER AND SWEETER.

1/4 cup mayonnaise

1 teaspoon grated lemon zest

1 baguette, split lengthwise

2 avocados, peeled, pitted, and sliced

2 plum (Roma) tomatoes, thinly sliced

1 cup (4 ounces) shredded pecorino cheese

2 cups watercress sprigs

Salt and freshly ground black pepper

In a small bowl, stir the mayonnaise and lemon zest together.
Spread the mayonnaise on both cut sides of the baguette.
Place a thin layer of avocado slices on the bottom piece
of bread. Top with the tomatoes, cheese, and watercress.
Sprinkle with salt and pepper. Place the other half of the
baguette on top and cut into 4 pieces with a bread knife.
Wrap in parchment paper and tie with raffia. *Serves 4*

Hummus and Pickled Onion Sandwich Wraps

THE PICKLED ONIONS CAN BE MADE AHEAD AND KEPT REFRIGERATED FOR A MONTH.
THEY ALSO MAKE A DELICIOUS CONDIMENT FOR ROASTED OR GRILLED MEATS.

1 cup Hummus (recipe follows)

8 oil-cured sun-dried tomatoes, drained and julienned

1 teaspoon minced fresh thyme

4 large fresh lavosh (Armenian flat bread) or flour tortillas

1 cup Pickled Onions (recipe follows), drained

8 red leaf lettuce leaves

To make the sandwiches, in a small bowl, combine the 1 cup hummus, sun-dried tomatoes, and thyme. Spread a layer on each lavosh to within 1/2 inch of the edge. Distribute 1/4 cup pickled onions over the hummus on each lavosh, top with a layer of lettuce, and roll. *Serves 2*

Hummus

1 (15-ounce) can chickpeas

2 garlic cloves, peeled

Juice of 1 lemon

2 tablespoons tahini (sesame seed paste)

1 tablespoon extra-virgin olive oil

1 tablespoon minced flat-leaf parsley

In a food processor, combine all the ingredients and blend until smooth. *Makes 2 cups*

Pickled Onions

2 pounds red onions, sliced

1 beet, peeled and sliced

2 tablespoons sea salt

1-1/2 cups white wine vinegar

1-1/2 cups water

1 teaspoon sugar

3 garlic cloves, halved

Place the sliced onions and beet in a bowl. Sprinkle with the salt, toss, and set aside for 1 hour.

In a medium saucepan, combine the vinegar, water, and sugar. Bring to a boil, then reduce heat and simmer for 1 minute, or until the sugar is dissolved. Set aside to cool.

Rinse and drain the onions and beets. Place in a nonreactive container with the garlic. Pour the vinegar mixture over. Cover and refrigerate for at least 1 week, or up to 1 month. *Makes 1 quart*

picnic baskets & boxes

3

Picnic Bento Boxes

THESE COLORFUL PICNIC BOXES ARE A VARIATION ON THE

CLASSIC JAPANESE BENTO BOX WITH A COMPARTMENTALIZED TRAY FOR FOOD.

BE SURE TO KEEP BOXED FOOD COOL UNTIL READY TO SERVE.

YOU WILL NEED:

Various sizes of plastic food containers with lids,
available at housewares stores
(be sure containers fit inside cigar box
with lid fully closed)

Cigar-type boxes with elastic band closure,
available at packaging stores

Paper napkins

Wooden chopsticks

Adhesive tape

TO MAKE:

Fill clean plastic containers with picnic foods and attach the lids. Arrange the containers in each cigar box and secure the lid shut by wrapping the elastic band over the top. Wrap a paper napkin around the narrow ends of each set of chopsticks and secure with a small piece of adhesive tape. Place a set of napkin-wrapped chopsticks under the elastic band on top of each box.

Decorative Picnic Takeout Containers

CARDBOARD TAKEOUT CONTAINERS COME IN A WONDERFUL VARIETY OF SIZES,
COLORS, AND PATTERNS. YOU CAN QUICKLY PERSONALIZE YOUR PICNIC
BY DECORATING THE CONTAINERS WITH THE COLORFUL ROUND LABELS
AVAILABLE AT OFFICE AND STATIONERY SUPPLY STORES.

YOU WILL NEED:

Assorted colors of round color-coding labels
(we used 1/4-inch and 3/4-inch sizes)

Cardboard takeout containers in assorted sizes,
available at container and packaging stores

TO MAKE:

Stick the labels on the containers in a decorative pattern,
varying the colors and sizes as desired. Fill the finished
containers with picnic food; close the top flaps and secure
the locking tabs.

Picnic Sand Pails

SAND PAILS ARE PERFECT CONTAINERS FOR PICNICS AT THE BEACH. GIVE EACH GUEST HIS OR HER

OWN PERSONALIZED SAND PAIL AND SHOVEL. WHEN YOU ARRIVE AT THE BEACH, THE LUNCH BAGS INSIDE

THE PAILS CAN BE EASILY REMOVED IF GUESTS WANT TO START DIGGING BEFORE THEY EAT.

YOU WILL NEED:

X-acto art knife or tweezers

Letter stickers, available
at arts and craft supply stores

Large plastic shovel

Plastic freezer Thermoses, available
at housewares stores and drugstores

Large plastic sand pail

Large glassine bags (8-1/2 x 15-1/2 inches),
available at paper goods and party-supply stores

Raffia

TO MAKE:

Using an X-acto knife or tweezers, lift the letters off the sticker sheets and write a guest's name with letter stickers in the center of each shovel and plastic freezer Thermos. Place the Thermos freezer inserts in the freezer several hours before the picnic to chill thoroughly.

Gently remove the handle from one side of each sand pail. Thread the pail handle through the end of the shovel handle, then reattach the pail handle to the pail. Repeat for each pail and shovel.

Pack the glassine bags with picnic food, placing the heaviest items at the bottom of the bag. Load frozen inserts into Thermoses and fill with juice or water, securing lids in place. Place the Thermoses in the center of the bags to keep perishable foods cool. Gather the top of each bag together and tie closed with a length of raffia.

Mother's Day Picnic Tea Baskets

INSTEAD OF SETTING A TRADITIONAL TABLE WITH CHINA AND LINENS, PUT YOUR MOTHER'S DAY TEA

IN A BASKET AND ENJOY THE LATE SPRING OUTDOORS IN THE GARDEN OR A PARK.

THESE FEMININE, PURSELIKE BASKETS WILL HOLD EVERYTHING YOU NEED FOR THIS SPRINGTIME CELEBRATION,

AND GUESTS CAN TAKE THEM HOME TO USE ANOTHER DAY AS A SMALL TOTE OR FLORAL CONTAINER.

YOU WILL NEED:

Scissors

Silk flowers

Small straw or woven purselike baskets with handles

Hot glue gun and glue stick

Card stock for name tags

X-acto art knife

Ruler

Hole punch

Decorative rubber stamp and colored ink pad (optional)

Pen

Plastic eating utensils

Paper napkins

Adhesive tape

Paper plates and cups

1-1/2 yards of 2-inch-wide organdy ribbon per basket

TO MAKE:

Using scissors, cut off the stem of each silk flower close to the head. Stick the end of a flower through a gap in the basket weave on one side of a basket and secure in place on the inside with a large spot of hot glue.

Cut out 2-by-3-inch cards with the X-acto knife and ruler and punch a hole in one of the short ends of each with the hole punch. Make a name plate on each card with the decorative stamp, if desired, and write the name on the tag with a pen.

Wrap a set of utensils for each basket inside a paper napkin and secure with a small piece of tape. Pack the wrapped utensils, a paper plate, a cup, and wrapped food into each basket. Tie the handles together at the top with an organdy ribbon tied in a bow. Thread a card onto one end of each ribbon, sliding the card all the way up to the bow knot. Repeat with the remaining baskets. Set a basket at each place setting just before serving. Guests can unwrap the baskets and take them home as a colorful memento of your Mother's Day picnic.

Hand-Stamped Picnic Boxes

CARDBOARD LUNCH BOXES, A GREAT WAY TO PACK INDIVIDUAL LUNCHES FOR A PICNIC

OCCASION, ARE INEXPENSIVE AND AVAILABLE AT PACKAGING STORES. HERE, WE DECORATED THEM

WITH COLORFUL HAND-STAMPED PATTERNS FOR THE PERFECT PICNIC LUNCH.

YOU WILL NEED:

White cardboard lunch boxes, available at
container and packaging stores

Rubber stamps

Assorted colored ink pads

White scrap paper for
practicing stamping designs

Pen (optional)

TO MAKE:

Leave the boxes unassembled so that they lie flat on the work surface. Practice creating stamped designs on the scrap paper with the stamps and ink. Try creating borders and patterns by repeating stamp designs and varying the colors you use. When you've created a design you like, repeat the design on the flat panels of the lunch boxes. You can stamp the design on all the sides and handles, if desired.

If you like, create a name plate on one of the side panels on each box and write a guest's name inside the plate with a pen. When the ink is dry, assemble the boxes by folding the sides together. Pack with food, a napkin, and eating utensils, and lock the handles closed by folding up the side flaps onto the notches at the top.

picnic barbecues

4

Grilled Prosciutto-Wrapped Figs on Gorgonzola Crostini

GRILLED FIGS ARE ALSO DELICIOUS WITH SMOKY SCAMORZE CHEESE OR CREAMY RICOTTA.

EXPERIMENT WITH YOUR FAVORITE FLAVORS.

12 fresh ripe figs

12 walnut halves, toasted

3/4 cup (3 ounces) Gorgonzola dolce latte cheese

12 slices baguette, each 1/2 inch thick, lightly toasted

Olive oil, for grilling

6 slices prosciutto di Parma, halved lengthwise

Light a fire in a charcoal grill or preheat a gas grill to 375°F. Brush the grill grids lightly with olive oil.

Make a slit in each fig without cutting all of the way through it. Insert a walnut half and a pea-sized piece of Gorgonzola in each fig, then close the figs. Spread the remaining gorgonzola on the bread slices and set aside.

Brush the figs lightly with olive oil and place on the grill. Cook for 2 to 3 minutes on each side, or until the cheese has begun to ooze out of the figs a little.

Remove each fig from the grill and wrap with a strip of prosciutto. Place on top of the prepared toasts and serve at once. *Serves 6*

Garlicky Barbecued Corn

NOTHING SPEAKS OF SUMMER MORE THAN
FRESH CORN ON THE COB. BRING THE BUTTER AND
GARLIC TO THE PICNIC IN THE SAUCEPAN,
THEN SET THE PAN ON THE GRILL TO MELT THE BUTTER.

6 ears of fresh sweet corn, husked

6 tablespoons unsalted butter

3 cloves garlic, minced

Salt and freshly ground black pepper

In a large pot of salted boiling water, cook the corn for 3 minutes. Drain and let cool.

In a small saucepan over low heat, melt the butter with the garlic. Set aside.

Light a fire in a charcoal grill or preheat a gas grill to 425°F. Place the corn on the grill, turning and brushing frequently with the garlic butter for about 3 to 5 minutes, until the corn is heated through. Sprinkle with salt and pepper and serve at once. *Serves 6*

VARIATION: Corn can also be grilled with the husks on. Soak unhusked ears in water for at least 20 minutes, then grill for about 5 to 7 minutes, or until the husks are blackened. Or, pull the husks back from the corn, leaving them attached at the end. Remove the silk and knot the ends of the husk to use as a holder and grill 3 to 5 minutes.

Grilled Salmon Fillets
with Pepper-Papaya Chutney

THIS CHUTNEY IS A WONDERFUL, TANGY ACCOMPANIMENT TO SALMON AND CAN BE MADE THE DAY AHEAD.
IN FACT, IT TASTES BETTER WHEN THE FLAVORS HAVE HAD TIME TO MARRY.

2 pounds salmon fillets

Salt and freshly ground black pepper

4 cups loosely packed baby spinach leaves

1 cup Pepper-Papaya Chutney (recipe follows)

Light a fire in a charcoal grill or preheat a gas grill to 425°F. Brush the grill grids lightly with olive oil. Season the salmon with salt and pepper. Grill for 4 to 5 minutes on each side, or until just slightly translucent in the center. Serve on a bed of spinach and top with a dollop of chutney. *Serves 4*

Pepper-Papaya Chutney

1/2 cup Champagne vinegar

1/2 cup granulated sugar

1/4 cup firmly packed light brown sugar

1 red bell pepper, seeded, deribbed, and cut into 1/2-inch pieces

1 papaya, peeled, seeded, and cut into 1/2-inch pieces

1 small onion, finely chopped

2 cloves garlic, minced

1 jalapeño chile, seeded and chopped (or more to taste)

2 teaspoons grated orange zest

1 teaspoon grated fresh ginger

1/4 cup minced fresh cilantro

In a large, heavy nonreactive pot, combine the vinegar and both sugars. Bring to a boil over medium-high heat, stirring often until the sugars are dissolved, then add all of the remaining ingredients except the cilantro, mixing thoroughly. Return to a boil, then reduce heat to a simmer and cook for 5 minutes. Stir in the cilantro and set aside to cool. Serve immediately, or cover and refrigerate for up to 2 days. *Makes 1 quart*

Mediterranean Marinated Swordfish and Shrimp Kabobs

CHICKEN BREASTS CUT INTO CHUNKS WORK VERY WELL IN PLACE OF THE SEAFOOD IN THIS RECIPE.

SERVE WITH COUSCOUS SALAD (PAGE 25).

18 jumbo shrimp, shelled

8 ounces swordfish, cut into 2-inch pieces

1 red bell pepper, seeded, deribbed,
and cut into 2-inch pieces

1 yellow bell pepper, seeded, deribbed,
and cut into 2-inch pieces

1 red onion, cut into 2-inch pieces

2 lemons, cut into wedges

18 dried bay leaves

1 teaspoon finely grated lemon zest

Juice of 2 lemons

2 teaspoons minced fresh thyme

2 garlic cloves, minced

1/2 cup extra-virgin olive oil

Salt and freshly ground black pepper

Soak 18 wooden skewers in water for 30 minutes. Drain. With a thin-bladed knife slice down the back of each shrimp, just deep enough to reveal the dark vein. Remove the vein and rinse the shrimp. Thread each skewer, alternating shrimp, swordfish, red and yellow peppers, onion, lemon wedges, and bay leaves. Place in a shallow dish large enough to hold all the skewers.

In a small bowl, combine the lemon zest, lemon juice, thyme, and garlic. Whisk in the olive oil. Season with salt and pepper. Mix well.

Set aside 3 tablespoons of marinade for basting. Pour the remaining marinade over the skewers. Let stand at room temperature for at least 1 hour, or cover and refrigerate as long as overnight.

Light a fire in a charcoal grill or preheat a gas grill to 425°F.

Remove the skewers from the marinade and grill for 4 to 5 minutes, turning frequently and brushing with the reserved marinade, until shrimp are pink and the swordfish is opaque throughout. Serve immediately. *Serves 6*

Grilled Halibut Packets with Tomato, Feta, and Olive Salsa

THIS FRESH SUMMER SALSA GOES GREAT WITH POULTRY AND MEAT DISHES AS WELL.

4 halibut steaks or fillets (about 6 ounces each)

Salt and freshly ground black pepper

TOMATO, FETA, AND OLIVE SALSA

3 ripe tomatoes, diced

4 ounces feta cheese, cubed

1/4 cup pitted kalamata olives, sliced

2 tablespoons salt-cured capers, rinsed

1 tablespoon minced fresh oregano

2 cloves garlic, minced

3 tablespoons extra-virgin olive oil

2 tablespoons finely grated lemon zest

1/4 cup dry white wine

Salt and freshly ground black pepper

Cut 4 pieces of aluminum foil and 4 pieces of parchment paper into 12-inch squares. Stack a piece of parchment on top of each of the foil pieces; place one piece of halibut in the center of each set. Season with salt and pepper.

In a medium bowl, combine the tomatoes, feta cheese, olives, capers, oregano, garlic, olive oil, lemon zest, and white wine, mixing until well blended. Season with salt and pepper.

Top each piece of halibut with a large spoonful of the salsa, dividing the mixture evenly among the 4 servings. Fold the foil packets in half, sealing the seams by folding over the foil edges twice to make packets air-tight.

Light a fire in a charcoal grill or preheat a gas grill to 425°F. Place the packets on the grill and cook for 20 minutes. Serve the packets on plates and let each guest open his or her own aromatic, steaming packet. *Serves 4*

Grilled Italian Sausage Skewers with Onion and Sweet Pepper

OTHER VEGETABLES, SUCH AS MUSHROOMS, ARE DELICIOUS ON THESE SKEWERS AS WELL.

WHEN USING VEGETABLES THAT NEED LONGER COOKING, SUCH AS POTATOES, BLANCH THEM FOR

A FEW MINUTES FIRST SO THEY CAN THREAD EASILY ONTO THE SKEWER AND WILL REQUIRE

THE SAME AMOUNT OF COOKING TIME ON THE GRILL AS THE OTHER VEGETABLES.

1 pound sweet Italian sausage, sliced into 2-inch chunks

1 small onion, cut into 2-inch pieces

1 red bell pepper, seeded, deribbed, and cut into 2-inch pieces

1 yellow bell pepper, seeded, deribbed, and cut into 2-inch pieces

Olive oil, for brushing

Salt and freshly ground black pepper

Light a fire in a charcoal grill or preheat a gas grill to 425°F. Soak 4 wooden skewers in water for 30 minutes. Drain.

Alternately thread the sausage, onion, and red and yellow peppers onto the skewers. Brush with olive oil and grill, turning frequently, for 12 to 15 minutes, or until the sausage has cooked through and the peppers are softened. Sprinkle with salt and pepper and serve at once. *Serves 4*

59

Grilled Hamburgers

THIS ALL-AMERICAN HAMBURGER IS SERVED WITH SLICED ONION, LETTUCE, AND SLICED TOMATO.
OTHER TOPPINGS TO CONSIDER: GUACAMOLE, BACON, SAUTÉED MUSHROOMS, BARBECUE SAUCE, OR CHILI. YOU MAY ALSO
OFFER A VARIETY OF CHEESES, INCLUDING SWISS, CHEDDAR, PROVOLONE, AND EVEN GORGONZOLA.

1-1/2 pounds ground beef

1/2 cup red chopped onion

Salt and freshly ground black pepper

4 hamburger buns

Mayonnaise, for spreading

1/2 onion, sliced

4 leaves green leaf lettuce

1 large tomato, sliced

Condiments
(such as catsup, mustards, and pickles)

In a medium bowl, combine the ground beef and onion. Mix well and divide into quarters. Gently shape into 4 patties, each about 3/4 inch thick. Wrap each patty in plastic wrap and refrigerate until ready to grill.

Light a fire in a charcoal grill or preheat a gas grill to 425°F. Place the patties on the grill and season with salt and pepper. Cook for 2 to 3 minutes on each side, or until browned. Continue cooking, turning every minute or so, for 3 to 4 minutes for medium rare, or an additional 2 to 3 minutes for well done.

Spread the buns with a light layer of mayonnaise. Top with the patties, onion slices, lettuce, and tomato slices. Offer additional condiments at the table. *Serves 4*

Split and Skewered Grilled Game Hens with Chili-Orange Glaze

BUTTERFLYING SMALL GAME HENS IS A GREAT WAY TO BOTH MARINATE AND GRILL THEM QUICKLY.

THE SPICY GLAZE GIVES THE HENS A WONDERFULLY PIQUANT FLAVOR THAT IS WELL SUITED TO A PICNIC BARBECUE.

SERVE WITH ROASTED NEW POTATO SALAD WITH PANCETTA-ROSEMARY DRESSING (PAGE 21).

4 Cornish game hens, rinsed and patted dry

2 mild dried red chile peppers (such as ancho or New Mexico chiles), soaked in 1/2 cup warmed chicken broth for 20 minutes

3 tablespoons extra-virgin olive oil

1/4 cup chopped onion

3 cloves garlic, minced

1 teaspoon finely grated orange zest

3 cups freshly squeezed orange juice

2 tablespoons minced fresh cilantro

Salt and freshly ground black pepper

With a large sharp knife, split the backbone on the inside of each hen lengthwise without cutting all the way through. Open each hen flat, like a book. Lace 2 metal skewers crosswise through the legs and breasts on the underside of each hen to hold the shape. Place in a shallow wide pan and set aside while making marinade.

In a blender, purée the soaked peppers and broth until smooth. Set aside.

In a medium saucepan, heat the olive oil, and sauté the onion and garlic for 2 to 3 minutes, or until softened but not browned. Add the orange zest, orange juice, and chile puree.

Cook over medium-high heat for 10 to 12 minutes to reduce and thicken slightly. Remove from heat; add the cilantro and season with salt and pepper.

Set aside 1/2 cup of the chile mixture for brushing when grilling. Pour the remaining mixture over the hens and let stand at room temperature for 30 minutes to 1 hour.

Light a fire in a charcoal grill or preheat a gas grill to 425°F. Place the hens on the grill and cook on each side 3 to 4 minutes, or until browned. Continue to grill, turning every minute or so, brushing with the reserved marinade, for another 4 to 6 minutes, or until flesh is no longer pink. *Serves 4 to 6*

picnic tables

5

Decorative Tablecloth Weights

BEACHCOMBING PROVIDES THE PERFECT SUPPLIES FOR THIS FUN CRAFT IDEA. USE THESE DECORATIVE

TABLECLOTH CLIPS TO KEEP YOUR BEACH PARTY TABLECLOTH ON THE TABLE AND NOT IN THE AIR.

YOU WILL NEED:

Electric drill and 3/32-inch drill bit

Medium-sized starfish, sand dollars, seashells, rocks, or pieces of beach glass

1 small skein hemp cord, available in jewelry and beading sections of craft supply stores

Drapery clips, available at fabric, upholstery, and linen supply stores

Scissors

TO MAKE:

Carefully drill holes in shells or starfish that do not have natural holes. Loop a doubled 6-inch length of hemp cord through the eyes of the drapery clips and pass the loose ends through the loop to secure the cord to the clip. Insert the loose ends of the cord through the shell hole and knot securely near the backside of the hole. Trim the excess cord with scissors.

For rocks and beach glass, use a 12-inch length of hemp cord, wrapping the object several times as if wrapping a package, both crosswise and lengthwise, securing the crossings with knots. Loop the loose ends through the drapery clip eyes and knot at the top of the clip.

Attach shell or rock weights to the corners of the tablecloth with the clips.

Flag Place Mats and Star-Folded Napkins

CREATE FESTIVE TABLE LINENS FOR YOUR NEXT FOURTH OF JULY PICNIC BY SEWING THESE SIMPLE STRIPED PLACE MATS. FOLD THE NAPKINS INTO A DECORATIVE STAR FOR EACH PLACE SETTING.

YOU WILL NEED:

Sewing tape measure

Sewing shears

1-1/4 yards 56-inch-wide printed red-and-white-striped tablecloth vinyl or oilcloth (makes 6 place mats)

Straight pins

Sewing machine

1 large spool dual-duty white thread

Six 20-inch lightweight cotton napkins, printed with blue-and-white star pattern

TO MAKE THE PLACE MATS:

Using the tape measure and sewing shears, cut six 18-by-14-inch rectangles from the vinyl or oilcloth, with the stripes going lengthwise. Miter the corners by cutting a 1/2-inch triangle from each corner. With the printed side up, fold under a 1/2-inch seam on all sides of the mat, pinning into place and at the corners to secure.

Using the sewing machine, sew the seams down by stitching 1/4 inch from the folded edge, removing the pins as you stitch. Stitch through all thicknesses of the overlapping corners on the underside of the seams as you turn the corners of the mat to sew. Repeat for each mat.

TO FOLD THE NAPKIN STARS:

Lay a napkin flat on a table, printed side down, and fold each corner into the center. Fold each corner into the center again.

Place one hand under the napkin and the other on top; turn the napkin over, holding the folded corners in place as you turn it. Fold each corner into the center again.

Hold the tips of the folded corners in place in the center of the napkin with the tips of your fingers. Gently lift each outer corner and tug on the flap underneath with your other hand. Repeat the process for each side. Place a napkin star in the center of each plate and crisscross a knife and fork on top to hold the center corners in place. Repeat to fold the remaining napkins.

Sand Shovel Napkin Rings

A PICNIC IN THE PARK NEAR A SAND BOX IS THE INSPIRATION FOR THESE DELIGHTFULLY SIMPLE SAND SHOVEL NAPKIN RINGS. YOU CAN PERSONALIZE EACH GUEST'S PLACE SETTING BY WRITING HIS OR HER NAME ON THE SHOVEL WITH LETTER STICKERS OR PERMANENT MARKER. IF YOUR PICNIC INCLUDES YOUNG CHILDREN, THEY WILL WANT TO PUT THE SHOVELS TO GOOD USE AFTER THE MEAL!

YOU WILL NEED:

Small plastic sand shovels

Letter stickers or black permanent marker

X-acto art knife or tweezers

Picnic napkins

Covered elastic hair bands in assorted colors, available at drugstores and beauty supply stores

TO MAKE:

Write the names of the guests on the spade end of the shovels with the letter stickers, using the X-acto knife or tweezers to remove and place the letters from the sticker sheet. Alternatively, use a marker to write the names.

Grasp the center of an unfolded napkin with your fingers and pull the napkin halfway through a hair band to gather the napkin. Slide the handle of a shovel through the hair band, with the spade end pointing towards the gathered point of the napkin. Repeat with the remaining napkins and shovels. Lay a finished napkin, topped with a sand shovel, at each place setting.

Beach Bottle Place Cards

CREATE YOUR OWN MESSAGE IN A BOTTLE AS A TAKE-HOME MEMENTO OF A PICNIC DAY AT THE BEACH.

YOU WILL NEED:

Tape measure

Small bottles with a neck opening at least 3/4 inch in diameter (we used an 8-ounce vinegar bottle)

Ruler

X-acto art knife

Map artwork, preferably with water and coastal areas included (we used an old U.S. Geological Survey map)

Beach sand

Sewing needle (must be longer than bottle corks)

Spool of lightweight fishing line

Small rubber fish or sea creatures (be sure they will fit through bottle neck)

Corks that fit bottle openings securely

Scissors

White kitchen twine

Decorative-edged scissors, available at fabric and craft supply stores

Pen

Hole punch

TO MAKE:

Using the tape measure, measure the circumference of each bottle and the height from the base to the bottle shoulder. With the ruler and X-acto knife, cut a rectangle out of the map paper that is one half as long as the bottle circumference and the height of the bottle below the shoulder. Roll the map gently into a tube and insert into the bottle. It should unfurl inside the bottle and create a backdrop for your watery scene. Fill the bottle with about 1/2 inch of beach sand.

Thread the needle with the fishing line, knot the end, and sew through the dorsal fin of a rubber fish or sea creature. Sew the other end through the center of the bottom end of a cork and pull the line through. Push the fish or creature into the bottle so that it dangles from its line, and set the cork tightly in place at the top. Adjust the length of the line to the desired length and knot the line several times close to the top of the cork to secure in place. Trim the excess line with the scissors.

With the regular scissors, cut a 24-inch length of kitchen twine and loop it around the neck of the bottle several times. Cut 1-by-2-inch nametags out of more map paper with the decorative-edged scissors and write a guest's name on the tag with the pen. Punch a hole at the end of the tag and thread the tag through one of the loose ends of twine around the bottle neck. Secure the tag and twine by knotting the loose twine ends at the bottle neck, and then knotting the tips of the twine ends to finish. Repeat with the remaining bottles.

picnic desserts

6

Minted Orange and Mango Salad

THIS REFRESHING SALAD CAN BE SERVED FOR BRUNCH OR AS A DESSERT.

YOU CAN SUBSTITUTE BLOOD ORANGES, IN SEASON FROM DECEMBER THROUGH APRIL,

TO ADD FABULOUS COLOR TO THIS DISH.

4 oranges

1 mango, peeled, cut from the pit, and cubed

2 bananas, sliced

1 cup sliced fresh strawberries

1/4 cup coarsely shredded dried coconut

1 cup vanilla yogurt

2 teaspoons finely chopped fresh mint,
plus a few sprigs for garnish

Peel, seed, and slice 3 of the oranges and place the slices in a large bowl. Add the mango, bananas, strawberries, and coconut. Set aside.

Grate 1 teaspoon of the zest from the remaining orange and juice the orange. Place the zest and juice in a small bowl. Add the yogurt and chopped mint and mix well. Add to the fruit and mix well. Garnish with mint sprigs and chill until ready to serve. *Serves 4*

Meyer Lemon Squares

AVAILABLE FROM OCTOBER TO APRIL, AND OCCASIONALLY DURING THE SUMMER,

SWEET MEYER LEMONS ARE THOUGHT TO BE A CROSS BETWEEN MANDARIN ORANGES AND LEMONS.

THE PEEL, ALTHOUGH IT IS QUITE THIN, IS DELICATE AND FRAGRANT, AND VERY GOOD FOR ZEST.

1 cup unbleached all-purpose flour

1 cup slivered almonds, toasted

1/3 cup confectioners' sugar

2 tablespoons cornstarch

1/4 teaspoon salt

6 tablespoons cold unsalted butter,
cut into small pieces

2 large eggs, lightly beaten

2/3 cup granulated sugar

2 tablespoons unbleached all-purpose flour

1 teaspoon finely grated lemon zest

1/3 cup freshly squeezed Meyer or
regular lemon juice, strained

3 tablespoons whole milk

Pinch of salt

Lightly butter a 9-inch square baking dish.

In a food processor, combine the flour, 1/2 cup of the slivered almonds, the confectioners' sugar, cornstarch, and salt. Pulse until finely ground. Add the butter and pulse to blend to the texture of coarse meal.

Press the dough into the bottom of the prepared baking dish and refrigerate for about 30 minutes, or until firm.

Preheat the oven to 350°F. Bake the crust for about 20 minutes, or until golden brown.

Meanwhile, whisk the eggs, sugar, and flour together in a medium bowl. Add the lemon zest, lemon juice, milk, and salt. Stir to blend well. When the crust is golden brown, pour the lemon mixture on top. Top with the remaining almonds and bake for about 20 minutes, or until the filling is firm. Let cool completely on a wire rack. Cut into 3-inch squares to serve. *Makes 9 squares*

Black and White Chocolate Brownies

TO MAKE A CHECKERBOARD PATTERN, ALTERNATE WHITE AND DARK BROWNIES ON A PLATTER.

DARK CHOCOLATE BROWNIES

12 ounces bittersweet chocolate, chopped coarsely

6 tablespoons unsalted butter

1-1/2 cups sugar

1/2 cup water

4 eggs

2 cups unbleached all-purpose flour

1/2 teaspoon salt

6 ounces bittersweet chocolate, cut into small chunks

WHITE CHOCOLATE WHITIES

4 ounces white chocolate, chopped,
plus 2 ounces cut into small chunks

1/2 cup sugar

1/2 cup (1 stick) unsalted butter

2 eggs

1-1/2 teaspoons vanilla extract

2 cups unbleached all-purpose flour

1/4 teaspoon salt

Preheat the oven to 325°F. Line two 9-inch square baking pans with parchment paper.

To make the brownie batter, combine the 12 ounces chopped chocolate, butter, sugar, and water in a small saucepan. Place over low heat, stirring constantly, until the chocolate is melted. Set aside to cool slightly.

Transfer the chocolate mixture to a medium bowl and whisk in the eggs. Stir in the flour and salt until blended. Stir in the 6 ounces of chocolate chunks and spread the batter in one of the prepared pans. Set aside.

To make the whities batter, combine the 4 ounces chopped white chocolate, sugar, and butter in a small saucepan. Place over low heat and cook, stirring constantly, until the chocolate is melted. Set aside to cool slightly.

Transfer the chocolate mixture to a medium bowl and whisk in the eggs. Stir in the vanilla, flour, and salt until blended. Stir in the 2 ounces of white chocolate chunks and spread the batter in the remaining prepared pan.

Bake the dark chocolate brownies for 30 to 35 minutes, until they pull away from the sides of the pan. Bake the whities for 25 to 30 minutes, until they pull away from the sides of the pan.

Let the brownies and whities cool in the pans on a wire rack for about 10 minutes. Loosen the sides with a knife or spatula and invert onto a greased wire rack. Cut each panful into nine 3-inch squares. Serve on a platter, alternating the brown and white squares to make a checkerboard pattern.
Makes 18 squares

Raspberry Scones

SCONES ARE DELIGHTFUL FOR A TEA PARTY OR BRUNCH.

FROZEN RASPBERRIES HOLD THEIR FORM BETTER THAN FRESH WHEN STIRRED INTO THE BATTER.

3 cups unbleached all-purpose flour

1/2 cup sugar

2 tablespoons baking powder

9 tablespoons cold unsalted butter, cut into small pieces

1 cup buttermilk

1 cup fresh or frozen raspberries

1 egg, beaten

1 cup fresh raspberries, for garnish (optional)

1/4 cup unsalted (sweet) butter,
at room temperature, for serving

Preheat the oven to 325°F. In a medium bowl, combine the flour, sugar, and baking powder. Mix well.

With a pastry blender or 2 dinner knives, cut in the butter until the mixture resembles coarse meal. Add the buttermilk and raspberries, stirring gently to blend. Turn out onto a floured board and pat until the dough holds together, handling it as little as possible. Divide into 4 pieces. Shape into rounds and score into fourths. Brush with the beaten egg. Bake for 30 minutes, or until golden brown. Serve with sweet butter and a few raspberries for garnish. *Makes 16 scones*

Banana Cake with Blueberry Sauce

THIS CAKE IS EASY TO MAKE AHEAD AND TRANSPORT FOR A PICNIC. WHEN SERVED,
IT IS TOPPED WITH A FRESH SUMMER BLUEBERRY SAUCE. THE SAUCE CAN ALSO BE MADE WITH OTHER
SEASONAL BERRIES SUCH AS STRAWBERRIES, RASPBERRIES, BLACKBERRIES, OR A MIXTURE.

1/2 cup (1 stick) unsalted butter, softened

1-1/2 cups sugar

1 cup mashed ripe bananas (about 2 bananas)

1/2 cup sour cream

2 eggs

1 teaspoon vanilla extract

2 cups cake flour

1 teaspoon baking soda

Pinch of salt

1 cup fresh or frozen blueberries

Blueberry Sauce (recipe follows)

Preheat the oven to 350°F. Butter and lightly flour a 9-inch square cake pan. Tap out the excess flour.

In a medium bowl, cream the butter and sugar until light and fluffy. Add the bananas, sour cream, eggs, and vanilla. Mix well.

In another bowl, combine the flour, baking soda, and salt. Mix well. Add to the banana mixture, stirring just until blended. Fold in the blueberries and transfer to the prepared pan. Bake for 45 minutes, or until a toothpick inserted into the center comes out clean. Let cool in the pan on a wire rack. To serve, cut into squares and serve on plates, topped with a spoonful of blueberry sauce. *Serves 6 to 9*

Blueberry Sauce

4 cups fresh or frozen blueberries

1/2 cup sugar

1/4 teaspoon ground cinnamon

1/2 cup apple juice

In a medium saucepan, combine all the ingredients. Bring to a boil; reduce heat to a simmer and cook for 10 minutes. Purée in a blender and strain through a sieve. Serve at room temperature or chilled. *Makes 3 cups*

Apple-Zucchini Cake

THE COMBINATION OF APPLE AND ZUCCHINI CREATES A DENSE, MOIST CAKE.

IT IS DELICIOUS AS IS WITH NO TOPPING, OR YOU CAN DUST IT WITH CONFECTIONERS' SUGAR JUST BEFORE SERVING.

2 cups unbleached all-purpose flour

2 teaspoons baking powder

2 teaspoons ground cinnamon

1 teaspoon baking soda

1/4 teaspoon salt

1 cup granulated sugar

1/2 cup firmly packed brown sugar

3 eggs

1/2 cup buttermilk

1/2 cup safflower oil

2 cups coarsely grated zucchini (about 3 zucchini)

1 cup peeled and shredded Granny Smith or pippin apples (about 2 apples)

1/4 cup walnut halves

Confectioner's sugar, for dusting (optional)

Preheat the oven to 350°F. Lightly oil and flour a 10-cup nonstick Bundt pan. Tap out the excess flour.

In a medium bowl, combine the flour, baking powder, cinnamon, baking soda, and salt. Mix well.

In a large bowl, whisk the sugar, brown sugar, and eggs together. Stir in the buttermilk, oil, zucchini, and apples.

Stir the flour mixture into the zucchini mixture, just until blended; do not overmix. Pour the batter into the prepared pan and sprinkle with walnut halves. Bake 1 hour, or until the cake pulls away from side of pan. Let cool in the pan on a wire rack for 15 minutes. Dust with confectioners' sugar just before slicing and serving. *Serves 8*

Red, White, and Blue Tartlets

THESE TARTLETS ARE A SUMMER HIT, ESPECIALLY ON THE FOURTH OF JULY. HERE, WE USED BOTH CONVENTIONAL SLICED STRAWBERRIES AND WHOLE *FRAISES DES BOIS*, TINY FRAGRANT STRAWBERRIES THAT CAN BE GROWN IN POTS OR IN THE GARDEN. THEIR STEMS, LEAVES, AND FLOWERS MAKE A NICE GARNISH.

2 cups graham cracker crumbs

1/4 cup sugar

1/2 cup (1 stick) unsalted butter, melted

1/2 cup heavy cream

8 ounces cream cheese, at room temperature

1/4 cup confectioners' sugar

1 cup fresh strawberries, hulled and sliced, or hulled and left whole

1/2 cup shredded dried coconut

1 cup fresh blueberries

Preheat the oven to 350°F.

In a medium bowl, combine the graham cracker crumbs and sugar. Stir in the melted butter. Press the mixture into six 4-inch round individual tartlet pans, dividing equally. Bake for 6 to 8 minutes, or until firm and lightly colored. Transfer to a wire rack to cool.

In a deep bowl, whip the cream to soft peaks and set aside. In another bowl, beat the cream cheese and confectioners' sugar together. Fold the whipped cream into the cream cheese mixture and spread in the bottom of the tart shells. Arrange the strawberries, coconut, and blueberries in 3 stripes on top of each tartlet. *Makes 6 tartlets*

Cheesecake with Brandied Cherries

THIS RICH RICOTTA CHEESECAKE, TOPPED WITH SWEET AND TANGY BRANDIED CHERRIES, IS A COOL FINISH TO A SUMMERTIME PICNIC. THE CHERRIES ARE ALSO WONDERFUL SERVED OVER A SIMPLE DISH OF FRESH RICOTTA OR VANILLA ICE CREAM.

2/3 cup sugar

1/3 cup unbleached all-purpose flour

30 ounces whole-milk ricotta cheese

5 egg yolks, beaten

1/4 teaspoon freshly grated nutmeg

2 teaspoons finely grated orange zest

1-1/2 teaspoons vanilla extract

Pinch of salt

Preheat the oven to 300°F. Butter and flour a 9-inch round spring-form pan. Tap out the excess flour.

In a large bowl, combine the sugar and flour. Add the ricotta, stirring just to blend. Add the egg yolks, nutmeg, orange zest, vanilla, and salt.

Pour the batter into the prepared pan and bake for 1 hour and 15 minutes, or until the top is golden brown and the cake is fairly firm around the edges (it will still be slightly soft in the center). Transfer to a wire rack to cool completely. Cover and chill well before cutting.

To serve, run a thin-bladed knife around the edges of the cake. Remove the side ring and cut the cake into 10 slices. Spoon chilled brandied cherries over each slice to serve. *Serves 10*

Brandied Cherries

1 pound fresh or frozen cherries, pitted

2 cups sugar

1 teaspoon ground cinnamon

3 cups spring or mineral water

6 tablespoons brandy

In a saucepan, combine the cherries, sugar, cinnamon, and water. Cook over medium heat, stirring frequently, for 5 minutes, or until the sugar has dissolved and the cherries have softened. Remove from the heat and stir in the brandy. Pour into a clean glass jar, cover, and refrigerate overnight, or up to 1 month. *Makes 1 quart*

picnic decorations

Fourth of July Centerpiece

YELLOW SUNFLOWERS AND A VINTAGE FOURTH OF
JULY POSTCARD WERE THE INSPIRATION FOR THIS FLORAL
CONTAINER. MIXING FLAGS AND FLOWERS MAKES
IT BOTH A PRETTY AND FESTIVE CENTERPIECE FOR AN
INDEPENDENCE DAY PICNIC TABLE.

YOU WILL NEED:

2-inch-wide foam craft brush, available at
craft and hardware stores

Small bottle of acrylic craft paint,
available at craft stores

Galvanized aluminum watering can or pail,
available at craft, floral supply, hardware,
or gardening stores

Small jar of matte-finish Mod Podge
(découpage water-based sealer),
available at craft stores

Vintage postcards or other decorative paper artwork
that will fit on aluminum container's side

Utility knife

Wet floral foam, available at
craft and floral supply stores

5 or 6 small 4-by-6 white-inch flags

Small bouquet of flowers in colors to complement
finished floral container

TO MAKE:

Using the foam brush and acrylic paint, paint the galvanized container on all sides and on the undersides of the handles. Let dry completely, for approximately 30 minutes, before applying a second coat if desired. Rinse the brush thoroughly in cool water and squeeze out excess water. Let the container dry another 30 minutes.

With the brush, apply an even coating of Mod Podge to the back of the postcard or paper artwork. Position on the side of the painted container and press gently to adhere. Repeat with more artwork on the other side of the container, if desired. In a thin, even coating, brush more Mod Podge over the artwork and the sides of the container to thoroughly seal the artwork to the surface. Let dry for 20 to 30 minutes. Apply a second coat, if desired, and let dry again. The Mod Podge sealer will be completely invisible when fully dry.

With the utility knife, cut floral foam to fit inside the galvanized container. Position the foam so that it is approximately 2 inches below the top edge of the can. Fill the container with water to the top of the foam. Arrange the flags in a circle in the container by inserting the flag sticks into the foam. Tuck flowers in between the flags in the same manner to finish.

Picnic Party Fans

KEEP YOUR PICNIC GUESTS COOL AT THE TABLE BY PLACING A DECORATIVE HANDMADE FAN AT EACH PLACE SETTING.

YOU WILL NEED:

Yardstick

Pencil

1 roll of printed wrapping paper
(a 2-1/2-foot by 5-foot roll will yield 8 fans)

Decorative-edged scissors (we used scissors
with a "corkscrew" edge), available at fabric and
craft supply stores

Plastic burnisher, available at art supply stores (optional)

Large stapler

Adhesive tape

Craft glue

16 colored jumbo craft sticks (2 for each fan),
available at arts and craft supply stores

Scissors

3/4-inch-wide ribbon cut into 24-inch lengths
(you will need 6-1/4 yards for 8 fans)

TO MAKE:

Using the yardstick and pencil, measure a length of wrapping paper 7 inches wide by 25 inches long. Cut out along the long sides with the decorative-edged scissors.

With the wrong side facing up, use the pencil and yardstick to draw light hatch marks 1 inch apart along both long edges of the paper to create the fold marks. Begin folding the paper into an accordion, using the hatch marks on the underside as folding guides. Make sure the first fold is folded with the printed side of the paper facing toward the outside. Press each fold firmly with the edge of your thumb, or use a burnisher to score the folds securely. When completely folded, mark the center of the accordion with a light pencil mark.

Staple the accordion layers together at the center mark, perpendicular to the long sides. Fold the accordion in half at the stapled center, scoring the fold firmly with your fingers or a burnisher. The decorative edges of accordion should now all be on the unstapled side of the fan. Tape the center panels of the accordion together with adhesive tape on the wrong side of the fan.

Open the accordion into a semicircle. Glue craft sticks to the wrong sides of the fan-end panels with craft glue. When the glue is dry, open the fan into a complete circle and tie the handles together with a 24-inch length of ribbon tied in a bow. Repeat to make the remaining fans.

Father's Day Party Ties

THESE EASY-TO-MAKE FATHER'S DAY TIES ARE A FUN PICNIC DECORATION THAT EVERYONE IS SURE TO ENJOY.

GIVE EACH GUEST A TIE TO WEAR WHEN THEY ARRIVE TO CELEBRATE DAD'S SPECIAL DAY.

YOU WILL NEED:

Black and white copy machine

Color photograph of Dad

Color copier

X-acto art knife

Sheets of 12-inch square colored
scrapbooking paper

Pencil

Ruler

Craft glue

Roll of 5/8-inch-wide grosgrain ribbon
(you will need 2/3 yard for each tie)

Scissors

Large letter stickers, available at
arts and craft stores

Glue stick

TO MAKE:

Enlarge the heart and tie template on page 109 by 200 percent, using a black and white copy machine. Enlarge an additional heart 300 percent for the heart frame on Dad's tie. Enlarge the photo of Dad's face on a color copier so that the head is approximately 1-3/4 inches high. Make multiple copies, one for each picnic guest, plus Dad.

Cut out an enlarged copy of the tie template using the X-acto knife and ruler. Lightly trace the template on the backside of a sheet of scrapbooking paper with the pencil, positioning it diagonally on the sheet to fit. Repeat, then cut out the ties using the X-acto knife and ruler. Fold over the flap along the dotted line at the top of each tie and glue down to the backside of the tie with a thin line of craft glue along the edge of the flap.

Cut a 24-inch length of ribbon with scissors for each tie and insert a ribbon through the ribbon flaps.

Using the smaller enlarged heart template, trace hearts with the pencil onto leftover scraps of scrapbooking paper and cut out with the scissors. Using the larger enlarged heart template, repeat the process to make one large heart for Dad's tie. Cut out faces from the color copies with scissors, silhouetting around the shape of head.

To decorate the ties, write "I love Dad" using the letter stickers, hearts, and cut-out faces of Dad. Position the elements running down the middle of the tie. Use a glue stick to glue on hearts and faces.

Rice Paper Candle Holders

GLASS FLORAL CYLINDERS, PERFECT FOR HOLDING VOTIVE CANDLES, COME IN A VARIETY OF SIZES.

COVERED WITH TRANSLUCENT RICE PAPER AND TOPPED BY A DECORATIVE PICNIC BUG, THEY MAKE A BEAUTIFUL CENTERPIECE

FOR AN EVENING PICNIC WHEN CLUSTERED TOGETHER IN THE CENTER OF THE TABLE.

YOU WILL NEED:

Tape measure

Glass cylinders, available at
floral and craft supply stores

Ruler

X-acto art knife

20-by-27-inch sheet of white or colored rice paper,
available at arts and craft supply stores

Glue stick

Matches

Votive candles

Decorative bugs and butterflies, available at
floral and craft supply stores

Hot glue gun and glue sticks

TO MAKE:

Using the tape measure, measure the height and circumference of a glass cylinder. With the ruler and X-acto knife, cut a length of rice paper the exact height of the cylinder and 1/2 inch longer than the circumference.

Apply glue along one short side of the paper in a 1/2-inch strip. Wrap the paper around the cylinder, lapping the glued side over the unglued side. Press firmly for 30 seconds to secure the glued seam.

Light a match and hold the flame next to the bottom of a votive candle for several seconds to soften the wax on the bottom. Quickly place the votive inside the center of the cylinder; it should adhere to the glass.

Attach decorative bugs and butterflies to the upper rim of the cylinder with a spot of hot glue if necessary. The dragonflies we used here have wire legs that can be hooked over the rim without glue. Be sure the wings and antennae are not near the flame when the votives are lit.

Repeat the process for multiple cylinders. Cluster them together with other votive candles in center of a table for a glowing table centerpiece.

picnic drinks

Iced Green Tea Spritzers

MAKE THIS TEA THE MORNING OF YOUR PICNIC AND CHILL WELL. IT GETS BITTER IF IT STANDS TOO LONG.

7 stalks lemongrass, tough outer leaves removed

1 cup water

3 tablespoons honey

3 green tea bags

2 liters sparkling mineral water, chilled

Ice cubes, for serving

Chop the white part of 1 stalk of lemongrass. In a small saucepan, heat the water to boiling. Add the honey and chopped lemongrass and simmer for 10 minutes. Add the tea bags and set aside to cool. Remove the tea bags and place the tea in the refrigerator to chill until ready to use. To serve, strain out the lemongrass and pour the tea into a pitcher with the sparkling water. Serve over ice with a lemongrass stalk for garnish. *Makes 2 quarts*

Honey-Orange Sun Tea

THIS CLASSIC FRUIT TEA CAN ALSO BE MADE WITH OTHER FLAVORED TEAS AND SUMMERTIME HERBS.

TRY MAKING IT WITH VANILLA-FLAVORED BLACK TEA, LAVENDER HONEY, AND SPRIGS OF SUMMER LAVENDER FLOWERS,

OR LEMONY EARL GREY TEA, LEMON SLICES, AND SPRIGS OF MINT OR LEMON VERBENA.

2 cups spring or mineral water, plus more as needed

1/2 cup orange flower honey

8 orange spice tea bags

1 unpeeled orange, sliced

In a small saucepan, combine the 2 cups water and honey. Heat, stirring, until the honey is dissolved. Set aside to cool. Pour into a 1-gallon clear glass container with a lid. Add the tea bags and orange slices and fill with cold water. Place in full sun for 2 to 3 hours, or until the tea is the strength desired. Remove the tea bags and place the tea in the refrigerator to chill until ready to use. *Makes 1 gallon*

Strawberry-Mint Lemonade

A BUBBLY LEMONADE CAN BE MADE BY USING SPARKLING MINERAL WATER.

1-1/2 cups sugar

3 cups water

1 cup loosely packed fresh mint leaves,
plus 6 sprigs for garnish

Juice of 6 lemons

1 cup coarsely chopped fresh strawberries,
plus 6 whole strawberries for garnish

2 liters spring or mineral water, chilled

Festive Ice Cubes (see note), or use plain ice cubes

In a small saucepan, combine the sugar and water. Bring to a boil and cook for 5 minutes. Add the mint leaves, lemon juice, and chopped strawberries. Remove from the heat and let cool. Cover and refrigerate until ready to use.

To serve, strain and discard the strawberries and mint leaves. Mix with the water. Serve over berry ice cubes and garnish with the whole strawberries and sprigs of mint. *Makes 3 quarts*

NOTE: To make Festive Ice Cubes, fill each compartment of an ice cube tray one-third full with water. Freeze. Remove the ice cube tray and place small strawberries, maraschino cherries, mint leaves, or little lemon slices in each compartment. Cover with water and freeze until ready to use.

Prosecco-Cassis Spritzers

CRÉME DE CASSIS IS A DELICIOUS LIQUEUR MADE
FROM BLACK CURRANTS. WHEN ADDED TO A GLASS OF SPARKLING WINE,
ITALIAN PROSECCO, OR CHAMPAGNE, IT IMPARTS A SLIGHTLY SWEET
FLAVOR AND ROSY COLORED HUE AND MAKES A REFRESHING APERITIF.

6 tablespoons créme de cassis

1 (750 ml) bottle chilled prosecco or sparkling white wine

Spoon 1 tablespoon of cassis into each of 6 Champagne
flutes. Add prosecco to fill each glass and serve immediately.
Serves 6

Sangria

THIS FRUITED WINE PUNCH IS BEAUTIFUL SERVED FROM
A LARGE GLASS CONTAINER. IF YOU'RE PICNICKING AT THE BEACH OR PARK,
STORE IT CHILLED IN A LARGE THERMOS UNTIL READY TO SERVE.
BE SURE TO CLEAN THE UNPEELED CITRUS FRUIT WELL BEFORE SLICING.

1 bottle dry red wine

2 cups freshly squeezed orange juice

1 peach, peeled, pitted, and sliced

1 orange, sliced

1 lime, sliced

2 cups fresh strawberries, hulled and sliced

1/4 cup sugar, or to taste

In a nonreactive 1-gallon container, combine all the ingredients. Let stand for at least 3 hours or refrigerate overnight.
Serves 4

Lime-Cooler Margaritas

THESE FESTIVE MARGARITAS CAN BE SERVED FROM A PITCHER BEFORE
AN ALFRESCO DINNER OR BARBECUE, OR TRANSPORTED IN A COOLER THERMOS AND
BLENDED JUST BEFORE SERVING FOR A PICNIC AT THE BEACH OR PARK.

1 cup freshly squeezed lime juice

1 cup freshly squeezed lemon juice

2 cups water

1-1/2 cups sugar

1/2 cup tequila

2 tablespoons Cointreau

2 limes, cut crosswise into 1/4-inch-thick slices, for garnish

Coarse salt or colored sugar, for garnish

In a glass pitcher or 2-quart Thermos, combine the lime juice, lemon juice, water, and sugar, stirring until the sugar is dissolved. Refrigerate until ready to serve.

To serve, add the tequila and Cointreau to the pitcher or Thermos and stir well with a spoon to blend. Rub the rim of each glass with a wedge of lime. Dip the rim into a small dish of coarse salt or colored sugar. Fill glasses with ice cubes and lime juice mixture and garnish glasses with a slice of lime.
Serves 6

Metric Conversion Table

LIQUID WEIGHTS

U.S. Measurements	Metric Equivalents
1/4 teaspoon	1.23 ml
1/2 teaspoon	2.5 ml
3/4 teaspoon	3.7 ml
1 teaspoon	5 ml
1 dessert spoon	10 ml
1 tablespoon (3 teaspoons)	15 ml
2 tablespoons (1 ounce)	30 ml
1/4 cup	60 ml
1/3 cup	80 ml
1/2 cup	120 ml
2/3 cup	160 ml
3/4 cup	180 ml
1 cup (8 ounces)	240 ml
2 cups (1 pint)	480 ml
3 cups	720 ml
4 cups (1 quart)	1 liter
4 quarts (1 gallon)	3.8 liters

DRY WEIGHTS

U.S. Measurements	Metric Equivalents
1/4 ounce	7 grams
1/3 ounce	10 grams
1/2 ounce	14 grams
1 ounce	28 grams
1-1/2 ounces	42 grams
1-3/4 ounces	50 grams
2 ounces	57 grams
3-1/2 ounces	100 grams
4 ounces (1/4 pound)	114 grams
6 ounces	170 grams
8 ounces (1/2 pound)	227 grams
9 ounces	250 grams
16 ounces (1 pound)	464 grams

TEMPERATURES

Fahrenheit	Celsius (Centigrade)
32°F (water freezes)	0°C
200°F	95°C
212°F (water boils)	100°C
250°F	120°C
275°F	135°C
300°F (low oven)	150°C
325°F	160°C
350°F (moderate oven)	175°C
375°F	190°C
400°F (hot oven)	205°C
425°F	220°C
450°F (very hot oven)	230°C
475°F	245°C
500°F (extremely hot oven)	260°C

LENGTHS

U.S. Measurements	Metric Equivalents
1/8 inch	3 mm
1/4 inch	6 mm
3/8 inch	1 cm
1/2 inch	1.2 cm
3/4 inch	2 cm
1 inch	2.5 cm
1-1/4 inches	3.1 cm
1-1/2 inches	3.7 cm
2 inches	5 cm
3 inches	7.5 cm
4 inches	10 cm

APPROXIMATE EQUIVALENTS

1 kilo is slightly more than 2 pounds.

1 liter is slightly more than 1 quart.

1 centimeter is approximately 3/8 inch.

Craft Resources

Pg. 38 (Picnic Bento Boxes): Cigar boxes and plastic food containers, the Container Store, www.containerstore.com and stores nationwide.

Pg. 41 (Decorative Picnic Takeout Containers): Takeout containers from the Container Store, www.containerstore.com and stores nationwide; color coding labels by Avery, available at office and stationary supply stores.

Pg. 42 (Picnic Sand Pails): Stickers, Mrs. Grossman's, www.mrsgrossmans.com or 1-800-429-4549; plastic freezer Thermoses, Cool Gear International, www.coolgearinc.com or 1-800-386-3374.

Pg. 45 (Mother's Day Picnic Tea Baskets): Baskets, flowers, and ribbon, Pine Street Papery, Sausalito, California; decorative stamp border, All Night Media, www.allnightmedia.com.

Pg. 46 (Hand-Stamped Picnic Boxes): Stamps and ink pads, All Night Media, www.allnightmedia.com; stamp patterns used are from the "Anna Griffin" stamp collection. Lunch boxes from the Container Store, www.containerstore.com and stores nationwide.

Pg. 69 (Flag Place Mats and Star-Folded Napkins): Tablecloth vinyl, oilcloth, and napkins, Jo-Ann Fabrics & Crafts, www.joannfabrics.com.

Pg. 90 (Fourth of July Centerpiece): Watering can, Jo-Ann Fabrics & Crafts, www.joannfabrics.com; vintage postcard, Susan's Store Room Antiques, San Anselmo, California, 415-456-1333.

Pg. 94 (Father's Day Party Ties): Letter stickers by Creative Letters from Making Memories, 1-800-286-5263.

Pg. 97 (Rice Paper Candle Holders): Stitched rice paper, Pine Street Papery, Sausalito, California; dragonflies, Laura Alders Handmade, www.lauraalders.com.

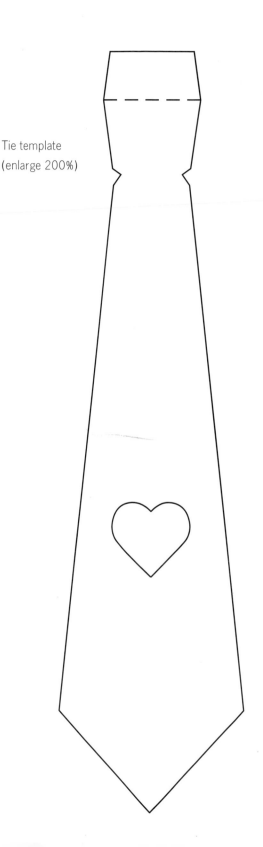

Tie template
(enlarge 200%)

Index